CHEMISTRY
in Your Everyday Life

Enslow Publishing
101 W. 23rd Street
Suite 240
New York, NY 10011
USA

enslow.com

Thomas R. Rybolt, PhD

This book is dedicated to my young grandchildren, Thomas, Harper, Olive, Joanna, and Ezra, who give us all joy, wonder, and hope.

Published in 2020 by Enslow Publishing, LLC.
101 W. 23rd Street, Suite 240, New York, NY 10011

Copyright © 2020 by Enslow Publishing, LLC.

All rights reserved.

No part of this book may be reproduced by any means without the written permission of the publisher.

Library of Congress Cataloging-in-Publication Data

Names: Rybolt, Thomas R., author.
Title: Chemistry in your everyday life / Thomas R. Rybolt, PhD.
Description: New York : Enslow Publishing, 2020. | Series: Real world science | Audience: Grade 5-8. | Includes bibliographical references and index.
Identifiers: LCCN 2018049679| ISBN 9781978507654 (library bound) | ISBN 9781978509450 (pbk.)
Subjects: LCSH: Chemistry–Juvenile literature.
Classification: LCC QD35 .R93 2020 | DDC 540–dc23
LC record available at https://lccn.loc.gov/2018049679

Printed in the United States of America

To Our Readers: We have done our best to make sure all website addresses in this book were active and appropriate when we went to press. However, the author and the publisher have no control over and assume no liability for the material available on those websites or on any websites they may link to. Any comments or suggestions can be sent by email to customerservice@enslow.com.

Photo Credits: Cover, p. 1 metamorworks/Shutterstock; cover, p. 1 (science icons), back cover pattern kotoffei/Shutterstock.com; cover, p. 1 (globe graphic) Elkersh/Shutterstock.com; cover, interior pages (circular pattern) John_Dakapu/Shutterstock.com; p. 5 Inna Bigun/Shutterstock.com; p. 6 Humdan/Shutterstock.com; p. 9 OSweetNature/Shutterstock.com; p. 11 3Dstock/Shutterstock.com; pp. 13, 20, 33, 39, 53 Thomas R. Rybolt; p. 16 KPG_Payless/Shutterstock.com; p. 18 Celiafoto/Shutterstock.com; p. 22 chromatos/Shutterstock.com; p. 24 Heike Rau/Shutterstock.com; p. 27 pixelman/Shutterstock.com; p. 30 snapgalleria/Shutterstock.com; p.32(top)DarrenPullman/Shutterstock.com; p. 32 (middle) fusebulb/Shutterstock.com; p. 32 (bottom) sharpner/Shutterstock.com; p. 37 Volodymyr Krasyuk/Shutterstock.com; p. 42 josefkubes/Shutterstock.com; p. 45 Jerry Horbert/Shutterstock.com; p. 50 Designua/Shutterstock.com.

Contents

Introduction 4

■ **Chapter 1**
Liquid of Life 8

■ **Chapter 2**
Oil, Water, and Soap 15

■ **Chapter 3**
Sugars, Sodas, and Diet 21

■ **Chapter 4**
Gases and Our Ocean of Air 28

■ **Chapter 5**
Metals 35

■ **Chapter 6**
Polymers, Plastics, and Fabrics 41

■ **Chapter 7**
**Energy, Carbon Dioxide, and
Global Warming** 48

Chapter Notes 55
Glossary 60
Further Reading 62
Index 63

Introduction

Whether you are in your home, at school, or in a store, look around you. What do you see? Lots of stuff. You may see a glass of water, bar of soap, metal coins, plastic bottles, books, or mirror with your reflection. These things are part of your everyday life.

Think about the many objects that people use every day. Plastics, fabrics, water, soap, oil, aluminum cans, soda drinks, oxygen in the air, and metal wires all have different properties and uses. Do they have anything in common? How can we understand what makes so many things that are so different? Scientists have learned something wonderful to help answer these questions. Scientists have learned that *everything is made of atoms.*

Chemists are the scientists who study how atoms behave and combine to make everything around us. Chemistry is the science that uses the properties and behavior of atoms to understand matter. All the stuff around you is made of atoms. So chemistry is the study of all the stuff in the world. Understanding something about atoms and ions, molecules, and chemical reactions will help you learn about the chemistry of your everyday life.

Atoms are the building blocks from which everything around you (and inside you) is made. There are 118 different types of atoms that are either found in nature or have been created by scientists in laboratories. Fewer than ninety of these types are found in nature in more than trace (very small) amounts.[1] Many of the artificial atoms made in labs exist in only small amounts and for short times because they are radioactive.

Introduction

Atom structure

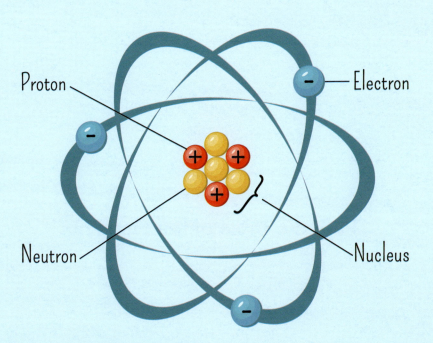

This representation of a lithium (Li) atom shows three protons and four neutrons in the nucleus and three electrons around the nucleus. The electrons would not really be in orbits but would be spread out to surround the positive nucleus like a cloud of negative charge.

Atoms are made of even smaller particles called protons, neutrons, and electrons. A proton has a positive (+) charge, a neutron has no charge, and an electron has a negative (−) charge. Protons and neutrons pack close together in the center of the atom, called the nucleus, which has a positive charge. The electrons in an atom form a cloud of negative charge that surrounds the positive nucleus.

Chemistry in Your Everyday Life

Each unique kind of atom is called an element. It is the number of protons in the nucleus that determines the type of element. Each element is represented by a one- or two-letter symbol. Some examples of different element symbols and their numbers of protons are hydrogen (H) 1, carbon (C) 6, oxygen (O) 8, sodium (Na) 11, chlorine (Cl) 17, and uranium (U) 92. A periodic table shows each element symbol and the number of protons (also called the atomic number).[2]

A neutral atom has no charge because it has the same number of protons and electrons. If an atom loses one or more electrons,

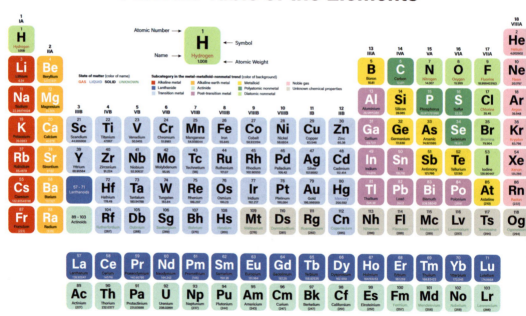

The periodic table provides a convenient way to organize the 118 known elements. It shows the element symbol, the number of protons in the nucleus, and much other useful information.

Introduction

it becomes positive. If an atom gains one or more electrons, it becomes negative. Positive or negative charged atoms are called ions. Positive and negative ions are attracted to each other. They can stick together to make a solid. Table salt is called sodium chloride (NaCl). It is made of positive sodium ions (Na$^+$) and negative chlorine ions (Cl$^-$).

It is hard to imagine just how small atoms are. Since they are so small, there are an incredibly large number of atoms in anything you can see. If you sprinkle table salt onto a dark surface, you will see many small grains of salt. On average, just one tiny grain of salt may have approximately 1,000,000,000,000,000,000 (one quintillion) sodium ions (Na$^+$).[3] That same grain would also have an equal number of chloride ions (Cl$^-$).

Molecules are collections of atoms that are held tightly together and stay together as a group. In chemical reactions, atoms or ions can combine to make new molecules. Existing molecules can exchange atoms or combine to create new molecules. Or a larger molecule may be broken down into smaller molecules. Iron rusting, a candle burning, and bread toasting are all examples of chemical reactions. In a chemical reaction, something new is created.

Liquid of Life

You drink it. You wash with it. You see it near the ground as fog. You see it in the sky as clouds. It falls from the sky as rain or snow. It is essential for life. What is it? Water.

Molecules at a Glance

The building block of water is the molecule H_2O. Atoms next to each other share a pair of electrons between them to form a chemical bond. The chemical bonds throughout the molecule hold the atoms together. Some molecules are found in nature. Other molecules are made by chemists who put atoms together in new ways. Millions of different kinds of molecules have been identified and studied! New molecules are being discovered and made every day.

Some molecules have many thousands of atoms, while others have just a few atoms. For example, carbon dioxide gas found in the air is written as CO_2. Each molecule of CO_2 has one carbon atom (C) and two oxygen (O) atoms. Table sugar is a molecule called sucrose, and its formula is $C_{12}H_{22}O_{11}$. Sucrose has twelve carbon (C) atoms, twenty-two hydrogen (H) atoms, and eleven oxygen (O) atoms held tightly together.

Molecules of Water

H_2O is made up of one oxygen (O) atom and two hydrogen (H) atoms held together by electron sharing to make two chemical bonds. The electron clouds around the atoms are negative, and the nuclei at the center of the three atoms are positive. This

Liquid of Life

collection of atoms with positive and negative charges creates a water molecule.[1] Water molecules are extremely small because they are made of only three atoms. To fill a one-liter bottle takes about 34,000,000,000,000,000,000,000,000 (thirty-four septillion) water molecules!

The tiny molecules of H_2O have amazing properties. None of us could live without water. Most small molecules of only a few atoms are gases, not liquids, at what scientists call room temperature (77°F or 25°C). For example, carbon dioxide (CO_2) and sulfur dioxide (SO_2) are gases at ordinary temperatures. Why is water (H_2O) a liquid?

Each water molecule has a slightly positive side where the two hydrogen atoms are located. It also has a slightly negative side where electrons are more concentrated. This distribution of positive and negative charges allows each water molecule to have a special attraction to up to four other water molecules. The slightly positive H atom on one water molecule can be attracted to the

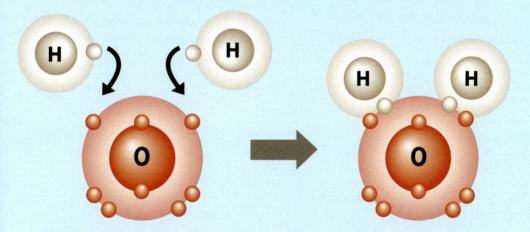

When a chemical bond holds two atoms together, the atoms share a pair of electrons. In water (H_2O), each hydrogen atom forms a bond with the same oxygen atom.

Chemistry in Your Everyday Life

slightly negative O atom on a different water molecule. This attraction is called hydrogen bonding. Hydrogen bonding helps hold the water molecules together despite their small size.[2]

As water boils, it changes from a liquid to a gas. You have to heat water to 212°F (100°C) to get it to boil. However, the larger sulfur dioxide (SO_2) molecule changes from a liquid to a gas at only 14°F (-10°C).[3] SO_2 does not have hydrogen bonding. SO_2 molecules are not held together as strongly as H_2O molecules.

Water for Drinking

Water molecules are pulled together by hydrogen bonding. The molecules wiggle, move, and bump together in constant motion, sort of like a crowded dance floor filled with people.

The special behavior of water allows other molecules and ions to dissolve and move around in water. If you add salt or sugar to a glass of water and stir, the ions of salt or molecules of sugar (sucrose) seem to disappear. Where do they go? They go into the water. They become surrounded by water molecules that keep them separated and hold them in the liquid. What was a solid is now dissolved in the liquid. We add sugar to make sweet tea. The tea is sweet because the sugar molecules are dissolved in the water.

You have to drink water because the human body is made of about 60 percent water (even more for children and infants).[4] So that means if someone weighs 100 pounds (45.4 kilograms), about 60 pounds (27.2 kg) of their weight is from water molecules. All cells in a human body are filled with water. The water allows the complicated biological molecules needed for life to be dissolved, to move, and to interact with each other. Water is found in blood and between cells. Water also helps keep the temperature of your body stable.

Liquid of Life

Tardigrades, or Water Bears

Water is essential for life. Humans die within a few days if they have no water.[5] However, there is a tiny creature, usually smaller than one millimeter, that can survive up to thirty years without water! These tiny animals are called tardigrades, nicknamed "water bears." They live in wet environments such as on moss and wet dirt. If the water around one dries up, it pulls its head and eight legs inside its body to make a ball. The chemical processes inside its cells continue, but go up to ten thousand times slower than normal.[6] Add water and the tardigrade goes back to its regular active life.

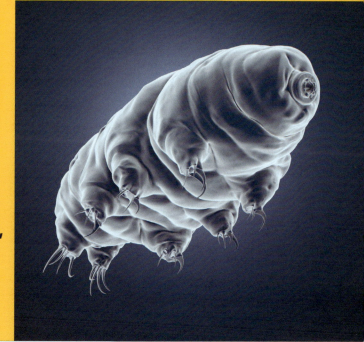

A tardigrade can survive for decades without water by going into a dried, nonactive state with extremely slowed chemical activity. When water is added, it can return to its normal activity.

Chemistry in Your Everyday Life

Clouds and Fog

Clouds and fog contain droplets of water. Sometimes, clouds are made up of tiny ice crystals. These small droplets or ice crystals scatter light. Light cannot easily pass through the cloud or fog.[7] For example, a light going through fog (droplets near the ground) is spread out in all directions. The fog looks white from the scattered light. It is hard for a driver in a car going through fog to see the road ahead. Clouds made from droplets in the sky also scatter light. Instead of the blue sky, you may see a patch of fluffy white. Clouds get darker and gray as less light is able to pass through them. When the drops in clouds become large enough, they fall to earth as rain.

Activity: Drops on Wax Paper and on Glass

Things You Will Need:

- wax paper
- a metal cooking tray
- a clothespin or chip clip
- blue food coloring
- a drinking glass

Obtain an adult's permission and help to do this activity.

■ **1.** Put a sheet of wax paper on a metal cookie tray, and hold it in place with a clothespin or chip clip.

■ **2.** Put one drop of blue food coloring on the wax paper. Blue food coloring is mostly water with some added dye molecules. We use food coloring because it is easier to see than pure water.

■ **3.** Raise one end of the tray until the drop begins to move. Observe what happens as you slowly raise one side of the tray higher.

■ **4.** Next, hold the open part of a drinking glass (made of glass and not plastic) facing you. Hold the glass so it is flat.

■ **5.** Add one drop of the same food coloring just inside the glass. Now slowly tilt the glass and observe what happens.

13

Chemistry in Your Everyday Life

Did you see the drop stay together as it rolled across the wax paper? On the glass, did you see the drop spread out into a long blue line? Why are they different?

The material that makes glass includes oxygen atoms. Water can form hydrogen bonds with these oxygen atoms in glass. Water is attracted to the glass and spreads across the glass surface. However, the wax paper has no oxygen atoms for hydrogen bonding. The water and the dye molecules (in food coloring) are attracted to each other but not to the wax surface. The molecules stay together as a drop.

Oil, Water, and Soap

Chapter 2

Have you ever heard the saying that water and oil don't mix? Oil stays with oil, and water stays with water. A molecule of water is polar because it has a positive and negative side. A molecule of oil is nonpolar because it does not have a positive or negative side. Polar molecules are attracted to water and are called hydrophilic (water-loving). Nonpolar molecules are not attracted to water and are called hydrophobic (water-fearing).[1]

Oil and Water

If you add oil and water to a jar, tighten the lid, and shake the jar, there will be a mixture of oil and water. However, once you let the jar remain still, the oil and water will separate into two layers. Some salad dressings have an oil layer and water layer, and you will see them separated. Even though you cannot see the motion, the individual molecules in a liquid are always moving around and by each other. However, the molecules will stay near the ones to which they are more attracted. One gallon of oil weighs less than one gallon of water, so oil's density is less than water's density. You will observe the oil layer above the water layer because oil is less dense than water.

Here is a way to help understand why the nonpolar oil and polar water separate into layers. Imagine a dance floor mixed with people where half are wearing green T-shirts and half are wearing blue T-shirts. Imagine the blue-shirted people want to be together, and the green-shirted people want to be together. If the blues and greens were mixed together at the start of the dance,

Chemistry in Your Everyday Life

Oil and water form two separate layers. Oil molecules are attracted to other oil molecules. Water molecules are attracted to other water molecules.

what would happen as the music continued? You would observe the blues coming together and the greens coming together. The dancers would become separated into two different groups—one blue and one green—just like the oil and water molecules separate.

Soaps and Detergents

Soap and detergent are examples of surfactants. Surfactants affect the surface tension or attraction between water molecules,

Oil, Water, and Soap

and they help water molecules spread out and wet surfaces that may have grease, oils, or dirt. There are many different types of surfactant molecules, with each having advantages for different types of cleaning. Surfactants have both polar and nonpolar parts so they can hold polar water and nonpolar oil together.

Clay vessels from ancient Babylon (dating back to 2800 BCE) have been found with writing on the side that says to boil fats and ashes together. These are simple directions for making soap. Inside these vessels, a soap-like substance was found.[2] At least some ancient peoples knew how to make soap almost five thousand years ago. We know from histories of the Roman Empire that

Maillard Reaction: Toast and French Fries

When bread is toasted, a chemical reaction occurs called the Maillard reaction. This reaction brings together amino acids in proteins and sugar molecules found in bread.[3] When toasting bread, the Maillard reaction causes the bread to turn brown. New flavor and odor molecules are made so toast tastes different from bread. Why do French fries taste different from boiled potatoes? The same Maillard reaction occurs in minutes at high temperatures (around 330°F or 165°C) when potatoes are fried in hot oil.[4] The surface becomes darker. New tastes and odors are created. However, in boiling water at a temperature of 212°F (100°C), the potato is not hot enough for the Maillard reaction to occur.

Chemistry in Your Everyday Life

Romans used soap for bathing and cleaning about two thousand years ago. However, the use of soap decreased and disappeared in many parts of Europe during part of the Middle Ages. The use of soap increased as people in the 1800s and in the 1900s realized its importance to help prevent the spread of disease and its use for comfort and cleaning.

Some ancient peoples made soap and used it for cleaning. Soap can be made from ashes, pure water, and animal fat or vegetable oil. Pure water, such as rainwater, and ashes can be used to produce a strong basic solution, which reacts with hot fat or oil to make soap molecules.

Oil, Water, and Soap

Soap is made from natural products by a reaction of animal fats or vegetable oils with caustic soda (sodium hydroxide, NaOH). The hydroxide ions OH⁻ from the NaOH react with the fats or oils to create new molecules. Soap has a positive metal ion like Na⁺ combined with a negatively charged fatty acid. A fatty acid molecule has a long chain of carbon atoms with attached hydrogen atoms to make the nonpolar part. It has a carboxyl group of COO⁻ atoms that make a charged polar end.

Detergents are made from synthetic molecules that ultimately come from petroleum (oil found underground and used to make gasoline, fuels, and other chemicals).[5] Manufacturers first created detergents during World War I, when there were shortages of soap.[6] This development continued, and today detergents are more widely used than soaps for washing hair, dishes, and laundry because they have many advantages. However, often people use the word "soap" more generally for any type of cleaning agent.

Activity: Moving Soap Molecules

Things You Will Need:

- a plate
- water
- black pepper
- dishwashing liquid
- a measuring cup

Obtain an adult's permission and help to do this activity.

■ **1.** Place a plate beside your kitchen sink. Slowly pour water into the plate until it is filled with water. Sprinkle pepper over the water until you see lots of black flakes on the water's surface.

■ **2.** Add just one drop of dishwashing liquid onto the center of the plate. What happens? Did you see the pepper move?

A soap molecule has a polar end and a longer nonpolar part. The polar side is attracted to the polar water. The nonpolar side is not attracted to the water. When a drop of dishwashing liquid hits the water surface, soap spreads across the surface. The polar end goes into the water, but the nonpolar end sticks up into the air. As the molecules spread across the surface, they push the pepper out of the way.

Sugars, Sodas, and Diet

There are many different types of sugar molecules found in nature. The white powdery sugar (table sugar) used in cooking and as a sweetener in coffee and tea is a molecule called sucrose. However, the sucrose molecule ($C_{12}H_{22}O_{11}$) is made of two smaller sugar molecules (fructose and glucose) that are linked together. When fructose and glucose link together with a chemical bond to form sucrose, they lose a water (H_2O) molecule.[1]

Two molecules can have the same formula but be different because the atoms are connected together in different ways. Fructose and glucose have the same chemical formula, but they are different molecules. Fructose ($C_6H_{12}O_6$) is found in many fruits. Glucose ($C_6H_{12}O_6$) is the primary energy source for our body and brain and is used in IV (intravenous) fluids.[2]

Complex carbohydrates such as starch are larger molecules made of many smaller simple sugar molecules linked together. Foods such as potatoes, bread, and pasta contain starches. Starch has a linear type called amylose and a branched type called amylopectin. When we digest food, complex carbohydrate molecules such as starch are broken down into smaller sugar molecules.[3]

Sodas and Artificial Sweeteners

Sodas can use sucrose as a sweetener but more often use high fructose corn syrup (HFCS). HFCS is made by the industrial breakdown of cornstarch into glucose and fructose along with small amounts of oligosaccharides (groups of three to ten simple

Chemistry in Your Everyday Life

Sucrose (saccharose)

The sucrose molecule (table sugar) is made of two smaller ring structures linked together. The rings are from two other sugar molecules called glucose (six atoms in ring) and fructose (five atoms in ring).

sugars).[4] Many foods sold in grocery stores have high fructose corn syrup added to increase sweetness. You can look at the list of ingredients on various bottles and jars to see what foods include HFCS.

Sugars, Sodas, and Diet

A typical 12-ounce (355-mL) can of non-diet soda contains about 39 grams of sugar (454 grams = 1 pound). If you drank one sugary soda a day for one year (365 days), you would have consumed 14,235 grams or 31.4 pounds of sugar!

Artificial sweeteners are molecules that have a much sweeter taste (hundreds of times sweeter) than the same amount of regular sugar (sucrose) or HFCS. Because they are so much sweeter, only a tiny amount is used, and there are very few calories. Some artificial sweeteners cannot be digested, so they have zero calories. Some of the artificial sweeteners used in sodas or other products include sucralose ($C_{12}H_{19}C_{13}O_8$), saccharin ($C_7H_5NO_3S$), aspartame ($C_{14}H_{18}N_2O_5$), and acesulfame potassium ($C_4H_4KNO_4S$). The sweetener stevia is a chemical called rebaudioside A ($C_{44}H_{70}O_{23}$) that comes from a plant. You can look at the ingredients list on diet drinks to see what sweeteners are used.[5]

Calories and Diet

The chemistry that takes place in living things is called biochemistry. Biochemistry can involve putting chemical pieces together or breaking chemicals (molecules) apart. Metabolism is the biochemistry of breaking down food and using this breakdown to create energy sources for a living organism.[6]

Dietary calories are a measure of the energy that people get from the food they eat. Teens and adults need anywhere from 1,800 to 3,200 calories each day. The amount you need varies depending on your age, sex, size, and activity level. In general, males need more calories than females, teens need more calories than adults, and more physically active people need more calories than those who are less active.[7]

Growing children gain weight as they age and get taller. However, once we are adults, our weight should stabilize. If an

Chemistry in Your Everyday Life

A chemical found in the stevia plant, rebaudioside A, has been estimated to be about 250 times sweeter than regular sugar (sucrose).

adult is at their proper weight, then weight loss can indicate too few calories and weight gain can indicate too many calories. On average, adult females need 1,800 to 2,200 calories and adult males need 2,000 to 2,600 calories each day. A serving of green beans may have only thirty calories, whereas a doughnut might

Sugars, Sodas, and Diet

History of Coke

In 1886, in Atlanta, Georgia, a pharmacist named John Pemberton developed a new drink. Some of the ingredients for this new drink came from the kola nut and the coca plant. Frank Robinson, a partner of Pemberton, suggested the name Coca-Cola for the new drink. During that time period, soda fountains in pharmacies would make and serve carbonated (soda) drinks. In 1894, Joseph Biedenharn set up a machine to bottle Coca-Cola so that people could drink it wherever they wanted. Pressurized CO_2 gas went into the water to make carbonated water, and the bottle was sealed so that the gas could not escape.[8] Today, hundreds of different kinds of carbonated drinks are bottled and sold in countries around the world.

have three hundred calories. Foods with lots of sugar and fat tend to have more calories. Calories are listed on food packages and often on menus in restaurants.

In addition to getting enough calories, we also need the right macronutrients, which include carbohydrates, protein, and healthy fats. According to the US Department of Agriculture (USDA), a healthy plate of food would be about 50 percent fruits and vegetables; 25 percent lean meat and proteins; and 25 percent healthy fats, such as olive oil and almonds. The USDA also recommends including some dairy products such as milk.[9]

Chemistry in Your Everyday Life

People also need micronutrients, which include minerals, vitamins, and phytonutrients.[10] Minerals include thirteen essential elements. Among these are iron (Fe) for oxygen transport in blood and calcium (Ca) for bones. Vitamins are molecules that our bodies cannot make, so we must get them from our diet. Vitamins are needed in small amounts to aid in certain biochemical reactions. Phytonutrients are compounds made by plants that have useful roles in human health. There are thousands of compounds made by plants, and scientists are still learning about the possible benefits of many of these.[11]

Activity: Carbon Dioxide in Soda

Things You Will Need:

- a balloon
- a bottle of soda (16-ounce size)
- a sink
- a pan

Obtain an adult's permission and help to do this activity.

■ **1.** Place a pan in a sink and fill it with hot water from the faucet.

■ **2.** Open the plastic bottle of soda. Immediately put a balloon over the top of the bottle.

■ **3.** Set the bottle in the pan of hot water. What do you observe? Does the balloon get larger? Do you see bubbles rise out of the soda?

Sodas are called carbonated drinks. Carbonated drinks are sealed after carbon dioxide (CO_2) molecules are forced into the liquid at high pressure. When the bottle is opened, the pressure is released and CO_2 molecules come rushing out. We see bubbles and we taste the fizzy liquid. In the liquid, all the molecules are close together. However, as a gas in the balloon, the CO_2 molecules are much farther apart and take up more space. The final volume of the CO_2 gas may be greater than the original volume of the sealed carbonated liquid.

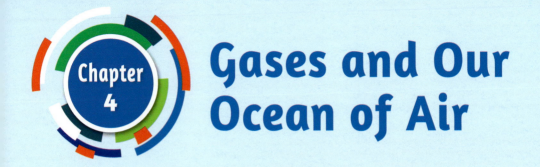

Gases and Our Ocean of Air

Did you know that you live at the bottom of an ocean of air? Just like an apple is covered by its peel, Earth is covered by a layer of air that we call the atmosphere. The atmosphere goes for miles above the surface of Earth, but it gets thinner as you go higher. Planes that fly at high altitudes (miles above the ground) have to pressurize their cabins because the outside air is too thin for passengers to have enough oxygen.

Air Is a Mixture

Air is made of a mixture of gases. Dry air (no water in it) by volume is approximately 78 percent nitrogen (N_2), a little less than 21 percent oxygen (O_2), and a little less than 1 percent argon (Ar). Another key molecule of air is carbon dioxide (CO_2), and it is about 0.04 percent of dry air. Air is essential for life on Earth. All animals need oxygen to breathe. All plants need carbon dioxide to construct the molecules from which they are made. There are small amounts of other molecules in the air called trace gases. Some examples of trace gases are ozone (O_3), methane (CH_4), and dinitrogen oxide (N_2O).[1]

Humidity

An important part of the air in different places is its water vapor or humidity. Water vapor is made of molecules of H_2O that are a gas and not a liquid. In a gas, molecules are far apart, moving rapidly, and constantly bouncing off each other (like billiard balls colliding). In a liquid, molecules are close together and moving

Gases and Our Ocean of Air

Tire Pressure

The air in the atmosphere is attracted to Earth by gravity. Near sea level, the air has a pressure (push per area) of about 14.7 pounds for every square inch (psi) of surface area.[2] Thin bike tires like those used for road racing can have gas pressures of 100 psi or more.[3] A tire gauge is used to measure how much higher the pressure is inside the tire than outside. The extra air in the tire helps to cushion the ride. Flat tires with no air would give us a bumpy ride.

around near each other. Humidity varies by location, weather, and season. Jungles have very high humidity. Arctic regions have cold, dry air and low humidity. The humidity is greater in the hot summer and lower in the cold winter.

Carbon Dioxide

Plants use the energy of sunlight in a process called photosynthesis. They convert CO_2 gas from the atmosphere into larger carbon-containing molecules. In photosynthesis, water from the ground and carbon dioxide from the air are combined to make sugar molecules such as glucose. Plants use glucose as a building block to make other larger molecules, such as cellulose and starch. In photosynthesis, plants produce oxygen. The chemical reaction for photosynthesis may be written as:

$$6CO_2 \text{ (gas)} + 6H_2O \text{ (liquid)} + \text{light} \longrightarrow C_6H_{12}O_6 \text{ (sugar)} + 6O_2 \text{ (gas)}$$[4]

Chemistry in Your Everyday Life

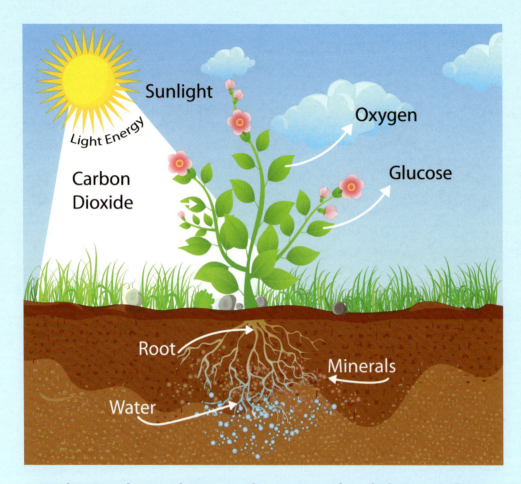

In photosynthesis, plants use the energy of sunlight to combine water taken in from roots and carbon dioxide from the air. This process is used to make more complex molecules such as glucose and also produces oxygen that is released into the air.

Animals that eat plants break down larger molecules into sugars and break down sugar molecules further to ultimately produce water and CO_2 molecules that are exhaled from the lungs. Plants use CO_2 to make molecules, and they give off O_2 that is then used by animals.

Gases and Our Ocean of Air

Oxygen

Antoine Lavoisier (1743–1794) was a famous French chemist who in 1789 wrote the first modern textbook on chemistry. Lavoisier measured changes in mass in chemical reactions and made careful measurements. Joseph Priestley (1733–1804), an English scientist, first isolated pure oxygen gas from the air in 1774. Lavoisier studied chemical reactions where oxygen was used up or produced. Lavoisier's wife, Marie Anne, worked with Lavoisier and was an important part of his laboratory work. She also translated some of his writings from French to English. Together, they learned that oxygen is necessary for animals, including humans, to breathe and for combustion or burning to take place.[5]

Lavoisier did many things to help French society, but he was involved in managing part of the tax system for France. During the French Revolution, royalty was eliminated and the king and queen were killed. Because of anger at the king and Lavoisier's tax work, Lavoisier was among the people killed (beheaded by guillotine) during the French Revolution.[6]

Oxygen is necessary for all animals, including humans, to live. Chemical reactions in our body need oxygen for energy. The red blood cells in our blood carry oxygen to all the parts of our body.

Oxygen is an essential molecule in many chemical reactions, including the browning of fruit and the rusting of iron. When you cut an apple, oxygen in the air reacts with chemicals inside the cells of the fruit to produce brown-colored compounds.[7] Iron (Fe) can combine with oxygen and water in the air to form rust. Rust is iron oxide (Fe_2O_3), with water molecules locked into the solid.[8]

Chemistry in Your Everyday Life

A fresh-cut apple turns brown as chemicals react with oxygen in the air. Our blood is filled with disc-like red blood cells. Just one red blood cell can contain more than 250 million complex hemoglobin molecules. Each iron atom in hemoglobin is able to hold, transport, and release an oxygen molecule. Iron combines with oxygen and water to form reddish brown rust.

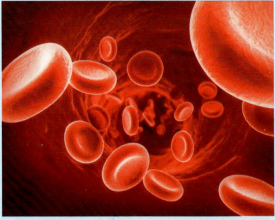

Activity: Air Pressure's Push

Things You Will Need:

- a microwave oven
- a measuring cup
- water
- an empty and clean plastic milk jug with a screw top

Obtain an adult's permission and help to do this activity.

■ **1.** Place half a cup of water in an empty one-gallon plastic milk jug. Place the plastic jug sideways in a microwave oven.

■ **2.** Heat the water in the jug for four minutes. The milk jug should be left on its side. The jug must be left open!

Chemistry in Your Everyday Life

■ **3.** After four minutes of heating, open the microwave, leave the milk jug on its side, and immediately screw the top on the jug. Be careful because the plastic will be hot. Make sure the top is screwed on tight so that no air or water can get in or out of the jug.

Watch the jug for the next five to ten minutes. What happens? When the jug is cool, you can remove it from the microwave.

When the water was heated, some of it was changed to vapor. As the water vapor filled the jug, it pushed some of the air out of the jug. After the top was placed on the jug, the water vapor cooled and returned to its liquid form. With less gas inside the jug, the pressure inside the jug was reduced. The greater outside pressure can crush a plastic jug.[9]

Metals

Metals are used in cooking pans, nails, mirrors, wire, coins, jewelry, bridges, cars, and in many other objects. Metals are used widely because they have many useful properties, including reflecting light and allowing the flow of electricity and heat. Some metals such as iron (Fe) and metal alloys such as carbon steel are strong, tough materials used in buildings.

Metals have many applications. Gold (Au) is used for jewelry. Copper (Cu) is used for wire. Aluminum (Al) is used in drink cans, automobile parts, and airplane parts. Lead (Pb) is used in car batteries. Lithium (Li) is used in rechargeable batteries for cell phones and laptop computers.

A glass surface coated on the back with a layer of silver (Ag) or aluminum (Al) can be used to make a mirror.[1] The shiny metal surface reflects light. The glass protects the metal from reactions with molecules in the air.

Alloys are made of metals melted together to have new and useful properties. Stainless steel is iron with at least 11 percent or more chromium, along with smaller amounts of other elements. Chromium makes stainless steel resistant to reactions with oxygen and moisture that causes regular iron to form rust.[2] Stainless steel is often used to make utensils (knives, forks, spoons), surgical equipment, and dental tools.

Electricity and Moving Electrons

A circuit is a path through which electrons can flow. Electronic devices, such as cell phones and computers, require extremely

Chemistry in Your Everyday Life

Mercury Thermometers

Mercury (Hg) traditionally has been used to make thermometers. Mercury is an unusual metal because it is a liquid over a wide range of common temperatures. Mercury atoms wiggle around and so take up a certain space. At higher temperatures, mercury atoms wiggle around more, move faster, and take up more space. The temperature scale is marked along the length of the liquid-filled tube. As the temperature increases, the liquid in the tube expands to fill more space.[3] Because of environmental and health concerns about the dangers of toxic mercury compounds, mercury is being used less and mostly has been replaced by other nonmetal liquids.

complex circuits and electrons that can move through them. A flashlight requires only a simple electric circuit. Moving a switch completes the circuit and allows electrons to flow from the battery through the bulb; light is produced. The metal wire in a flashlight circuit allows electrons to flow easily.

A metal is made of positive atoms called cations that are in fixed positions and negative free electrons that are able to move through the solid. The negative electrons hold the positive cations together because electrical opposites (positive and negative) attract each other.

Metal is an excellent electrical conductor. As electrons are pushed into one end of a wire, the free electrons (electricity) can move through the solid metal wire. Using a battery to power a circuit, electrons leave the negative end of the battery, flow

Metals

Modern electronic devices use "chips" with integrated circuits that may contain billions of transistors, which control the flow of electricity. Integrated circuit chips are "printed" onto a surface like silicon (Si) in a process using light called photolithography. These chips are an essential part of electronic circuits in computers, cell phones, and many other devices.

through the circuit, and return to the positive end. Metals have free electrons in their structure. These electrons are not locked into fixed positions and are free to flow through a metal.[4]

In plastic solids, electrons are locked into position within each molecule. The electrons cannot move through the solid. Plastics are poor conductors of electricity. A material that is a poor conductor of electricity is called an electrical insulator.[5]

Copper (Cu) wire is used to provide the wiring for homes, offices, factories, and schools. However, the copper metal is surrounded by a plastic or rubber-like material. The copper wire conducts the electricity, but it must be covered with an outer part that is an insulator. Since the copper conducts electricity, it would not be safe to use if it was not covered by an insulator.

Conducting Heat

Materials that allow heat to pass easily through them are called thermal conductors. Materials that do not allow this easy flow of heat are called thermal insulators. Metals are good conductors of heat. Plastics are not good conductors of heat.

Scientists have learned that heat energy is the energy of random motion. Atoms in a solid vibrate, or move back and forth. The higher the temperature, the greater this atomic motion is in a solid. If heat is added to a solid, the atoms in the solid will vibrate or move more rapidly, and the temperature will increase. Faster vibrating atoms in a metal bump into other nearby atoms and cause them to vibrate more rapidly. As heat passes through a metal, the atoms are able to vibrate faster and pass this motion on to nearby atoms.[6]

Plastic is made up of large molecules called polymers that are locked into fixed positions. Because they are not able to move as easily, they can't conduct heat through the solid. Styrofoam is a general term that refers to the expanded lightweight polystyrene plastic used in coolers because it is an insulator. It helps keep heat out so that whatever is inside stays cold.[7]

Activity: Heat Flow Through Metal and Plastic

Things You Will Need:

- 2 glasses
- a sink faucet for cool and hot water
- ice
- 2 plastic spoons
- 2 metal spoons
- a watch or clock

Obtain an adult's permission and help to do this activity.

■ **1.** Fill the first glass with ice cubes and add water to near the top of the glass.

Chemistry in Your Everyday Life

■ **2.** Turn on a sink faucet and let the hot water run until it is as hot as possible. Fill the second glass to near the top with this hot water.

■ **3.** Place a plastic and a metal spoon into each glass. Wait about eight minutes and touch the part of the spoon that is out of the water. Compare the temperature of each spoon.

The metal spoons were probably colder and hotter than the plastic spoons because metal is an excellent conductor of heat. Heat spreads from the hot water into and through the metal spoon. In the ice water, heat moved from the end of the metal spoon sticking out of the water into the cold water. As the heat moved into the cold water, the other part of the spoon got colder.

Plastic is not a good conductor of heat, so the temperature of the plastic spoons probably did not change much.

Polymers, Plastics, and Fabrics

Chapter 6

Polymers are very large molecules made up of many small molecules linked together. The small molecules are called monomers. Since "poly" means many, then many monomers together make a "polymer." There are natural polymers, such as cellulose, proteins, DNA, and starch. There also are synthetic polymers, which do not exist in nature.[1]

If a paper clip represented some molecule, a polymer would be like a long chain of paper clips all hooked together. In some polymers, there is one long chain. In other polymers, there are many smaller branches of chains coming off the longest main chain. Polymers may be made up of thousands of small molecules linked together. The properties of polymers depend on the specific monomer molecules used, the amount of branching, the size of the final polymer molecules, and the way the polymer molecules line up. The chemical reaction used to make a polymer is called polymerization. Often, different polymers are mixed together to adjust the properties.

The first synthetic polymer was made in 1907. This polymer was called Bakelite after the American chemist, Leo Baekeland (1863–1944), who developed it. It was a good insulator and developed many early uses, including cases for radios and telephones, billiard balls, children's toys, game pieces, and even jewelry.[2] Bakelite was the start of the modern plastic industry that continues today.

There are thousands of types of objects made of polymers, but the names of polymers generally refer back to the small molecules used to make them. Polycarbonate (Lexan) is a tough, transparent

Chemistry in Your Everyday Life

The first synthetic polymer was Bakelite. Early Bakelite radios were brown or black because of the heating process used to make the final plastic shape.

material used to make shatterproof windows or eyeglass lenses. Polyamides (nylons) of different types are used for strong fibers, ropes, and clothing. One of the first uses of nylon (1940) was in stockings. Polypropylene is used to make dishwasher-safe dishes. Polyvinyl chloride (PVC) is used to make plumbing pipes.[3]

Plastics

Plastic is any type of material made up of large polymers that can be molded into useful shapes. Plastics can be molded to make

Polymers, Plastics, and Fabrics

bottles, straws, fibers, car parts, toys, and many different objects. Recycled plastic can be heated to soften and then forced into the desired shape. When the plastic cools, the shape is locked into place.[4]

Thermoplastics are materials that can be melted and reshaped into new objects. Number codes are placed on many plastic objects to help identify them for recycling. Some of the most commonly used thermoplastics and their codes are polyethylene terephthalate (1, PETE), used to make bottles for carbonated drinks; high-density polyethylene (2, HDPE), used to make milk jugs; and low-density polyethylene (4, LDPE), used to make plastic bags.[5]

Thermoset plastics undergo a chemical reaction when made. They can't be reshaped once they are formed.[6] For example, the vulcanization of rubber is a process where rubber is heated with sulfur so that each sulfur atom can link different chains of rubber together. After years of work, by 1842, Charles Goodyear (1800–1860) developed this process using natural rubber.[7] Having these sulfur links improves the properties of rubber, but it can't be heated and reshaped. Because of the bonds between all the atoms, a thermoset material is like one giant molecule. Hard plastic buttons are usually made of a thermoset plastic.

Fibers: Cotton and Polyester

Clothes are made from fabrics cut into pieces and sewn together. Fabric is a cloth material made from woven threads. These threads can be made from natural or synthetic fibers. Natural fibers include silk, wool, and cotton. Synthetic fibers include nylon, polyester, and polyacrylonitrile.[8]

In cotton plants, fluffy white cotton cellulose fibers form in clumps around the seeds. After these clumps of cotton are picked,

Chemistry in Your Everyday Life

An Ocean of Plastics

Because plastic is inexpensive, it has been used for bottles, packaging, bags, and many other purposes. Because plastic is cheap, a lot of it is used once, such as single-use water bottles, and then thrown away. Around the world, discarded plastic is creating enormous waste. It has been estimated that as much as 19 billion pounds (8.6 billion kg) of plastic trash ends up in the ocean each year. Because plastic is non-biodegradable, it tends to simply break down into smaller and smaller pieces called microplastics. It has been estimated that there are trillions of tiny microplastic particles in seas.[9] Both large and tiny plastic trash may be harmful to the marine environment and aquatic life.

the seeds are removed from the white fibers in a process called ginning. Cotton fibers are 90 percent cellulose—the purest found in nature. After processing, the fibers are spun into threads that can be used to make cloth for clothing.[10]

Cotton and polyester are both polymers that are widely used for making clothes. Cotton is grown on farms, and polyester is a synthetic fiber manufactured at industrial chemical plants. Globally, billions of pounds of cotton and polyester are produced and used every year.

After solid polyester is made, it is cut into pieces that are melted and forced through tiny holes called spinnerets to make

Polymers, Plastics, and Fabrics

The fluffy, white clumps of fiber that grow on cotton plants are called bolls. The bolls protect the seeds.

Chemistry in Your Everyday Life

long fibers. The polyester fiber is stretched to make longer and thinner thread.[11]

    Cotton makes strong fibers and comfortable fabric, but it can wrinkle easily without additional processing. Cotton readily absorbs water. Polyester is more water-resistant than cotton. Sometimes, cotton is blended with polyester to create improved properties, such as being wrinkle-resistant. Look at the tags on some clothes to find ones that are cotton, polyester, or a cotton/polyester blend. Compare how they look and feel.

Activity: Cotton and Polyester Water Retention

Things You Will Need:

- a cotton shirt
- a polyester or polyester blend shirt
- a watch or clock
- a sink faucet

Obtain an adult's permission and help to do this activity.

■ **1.** Run water from a faucet to thoroughly wet about 6 inches (15 centimeters) of one of the sleeves of a cotton shirt and a polyester or polyester/cotton blend shirt.

■ **2.** Hang each shirt over a sink so that the sleeve is open to the air (not covered). Look at a watch or clock and observe the time.

■ **3.** Touch each wet sleeve and write down how they feel.

■ **4.** Touch the sleeves again in a half hour and repeat each half hour. You may need to continue feeling the sleeves every half hour for three to five hours. Does one shirt stay wetter for longer?

Cotton has many oxygen atoms with which the water can form hydrogen bonds and be attracted, so you will probably find that the cotton feels wetter longer.

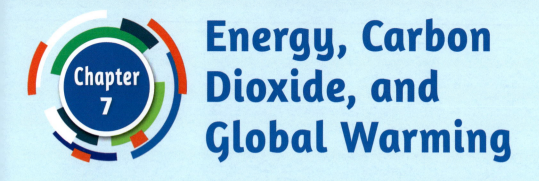

Energy, Carbon Dioxide, and Global Warming

Fire is the result of a chemical reaction called combustion in which new molecules are formed and heat and light are produced. Fuel (such as wood) and oxygen from the air are both needed.[1] Wood contains large, complex molecules, such as cellulose and lignin, made of carbon, hydrogen, and oxygen atoms. At high temperatures, these and other carbon-containing molecules are broken apart and combine with oxygen (O_2) to produce hot gas molecules of carbon dioxide (CO_2) and water (H_2O). Metals in the wood combine with oxygen to form the ash that is left behind.[2]

Over the last two hundred years or so, fuel sources other than wood have been developed, including coal, oil, gasoline, diesel fuel, and natural gas (methane CH_4).[3] All of these fossil fuels include molecules that contain carbon (C) and hydrogen (H) atoms. When fossil fuels are burned, carbon (C) atoms combine with O_2, CO_2 is produced, and CO_2 gas goes into Earth's atmosphere.

Some of the CO_2 gas goes from the atmosphere into the ocean. Carbon dioxide from the atmosphere dissolves in the surface waters of the ocean. Photosynthesis by phytoplankton organisms uses some of the CO_2, and other marine organisms make calcium carbonate $CaCO_3$ as part of their shells and skeletons.[4] Some of this trapped carbon settles to the bottom of the ocean.

When CO_2 gas dissolves into ocean water, some of the CO_2 molecules can combine with H_2O to form carbonic acid H_2CO_3 that with another H_2O makes H_3O^+ (hydronium) and HCO_3^- (bicarbonate) ions. H_3O^+ makes water acidic. Over the last two hundred years, the ocean has become more acidic. An increase in acid can be harmful to plants and animals that live in the ocean.[5]

Carbon Dioxide and Global Warming

A parked car with all its windows closed can get dangerously hot in the summer. The temperature increases because the heat cannot escape. A greenhouse made of glass or plastic is used to trap heat and keep plants warm in the winter. The trapping of heat at Earth's surface, on land, and in the oceans is called the greenhouse effect.[6] The carbon dioxide that does not go into the ocean builds up in the atmosphere because more CO_2 is put into the air than can be used by plants in photosynthesis. CO_2 is a greenhouse gas that traps heat that would otherwise leave Earth and go out into space.

Carbon Dioxide in the Atmosphere

Scientists have been measuring the amount of CO_2 in the atmosphere on a mountain in Hawaii called Mauna Loa continuously since 1958. Now it is measured at many places around the world. The amount of carbon dioxide gas in Earth's atmosphere was 315 parts per million (ppm) in 1960, 350 ppm in 1990, and 400 ppm in 2018. The measurement 400 ppm means that out of one million different molecules in the air, four hundred are CO_2. While this change may not seem large, it is a leading cause of global warming.[7]

Chemistry in Your Everyday Life

Greenhouse effect

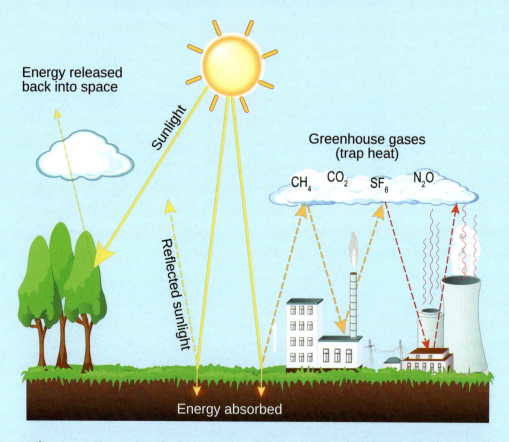

The sun warms Earth, but some of that heat is radiated or released back into space. Increasing greenhouse gases in the atmosphere can trap too much heat and cause our planet to get warmer.

The surface of Earth is warmed by the sun. However, some of that heat goes back into the atmosphere and into outer space. Heat is trapped by water, carbon dioxide, methane, and certain other greenhouse gases in the atmosphere. The presence of H_2O

and CO_2 in the atmosphere can help Earth from being too cold. However, the balance in nature is being changed in a dangerous way because of the increase of CO_2 and other greenhouse gases, such as methane (CH_4). The increase in trapped heat is causing a slow but steady increase in Earth's average temperature. This is known as global warming.[8]

Global warming leads to melting glaciers and polar ice, increases in sea level, and storms and rain that increase flooding of coastal towns and cities. Global warming changes weather patterns resulting in increases in rain and flooding in some areas and lack of rain, more wildfires, and crops dying in other places. Global warming contributes to a warmer ocean that causes more extreme (wetter and windy) and destructive hurricanes. New record-high temperatures are observed every year, and periods of extreme summer heat can be a significant health risk.

Global Challenge

There is a great challenge ahead for all people. We continue to need energy sources to run our homes, businesses, farms, factories, trains, cars, trucks, and planes. However, we need sources of energy that do not put large amounts of carbon dioxide gas into the atmosphere. We need sources of energy that do not require burning carbon-containing molecules to produce heat energy.

Humans need to utilize more alternative sources, such as wind, solar, and hydroelectric, as well as the energy trapped inside the nuclei of atoms. People need to continue to find ways to use energy efficiently. For example, better insulation for homes and businesses can reduce energy usage. We can produce more cars and trucks that utilize batteries and more efficient electric motors instead of combustion engines that burn gasoline.

Chemistry in Your Everyday Life

To avoid a warming world and a damaged ocean, people around the world need the courage to face the challenges ahead. Whether you help as a scientist, an engineer, or an active citizen, a knowledge of atoms, molecules, and chemical reactions will help you along the way.

Activity: The Greenhouse Effect

Things You Will Need:

- 2 large, empty glass jars (canning jars sold in grocery stores work well)
- plain white paper
- a watch
- an outdoor thermometer (These thermometers have a temperature scale marked on a piece of metal and a tube filled with a colored liquid next to the scale.)

Obtain an adult's permission and help to do this activity.

■ **1.** Go outside on a bright sunny day, put the thermometer in the shade, wait ten minutes, and observe the air temperature using the scale on the thermometer.

■ **2.** Place several pieces of white paper on a flat surface where the sun is shining. Put an open jar on top of this paper.

■ **3.** Place the thermometer into the jar where it sticks out of the top of the jar. Place a second jar upside down on top of the first jar so that the thermometer is completely inside the two jars. The jars must be touching.

53

Chemistry in Your Everyday Life

■ **4.** Use a watch or timer and write down the time and temperature every five minutes. Continue until the temperature stops changing. Can you describe what you observed? Glass can trap heat and cause greenhouse warming. Did you observe an increase in the temperature when the jars were together and the heat was trapped inside?

Introduction

1. Anne Marie Helmenstine, "How Many Elements Can Be Found Naturally?" ThoughtCo., January 31, 2018, https://www.thoughtco.com/how-many-elements-found-naturally-606636.
2. "Interactive Periodic Table," PTable, accessed October 9, 2018, https://www.ptable.com.
3. Yasar Safkan, "How Many Atoms Are in a Grain of Salt?" PhysLink.com, accessed September 6, 2018, http://www4.hcmut.edu.vn/~huynhqlinh/olympicvl/tailieu/physlink_askexpert/ae342.cfm.htm.

■ Chapter 1
Liquid of Life

1. Nivaldo J. Tro, *Chemistry Structure and Properties 2nd Edition* (Hoboken, NJ: Pearson, 2018), p. 36.
2. Martin Chaplin, "Hydrogen Bonding in Water," Water Structure and Science, accessed August 7, 2018, http://www1.lsbu.ac.uk/water/water_hydrogen_bonding.html.
3. "Sulfur Dioxide," CAMEO Chemicals, accessed November 15, 2018, https://cameochemicals.noaa.gov/chemical/1554.
4. Anne Marie Helmenstine, "How Much of Your Body Is Water?" ThoughtCo., June 1, 2018, accessed August 7, 2018, https://www.thoughtco.com/how-much-of-your-body-is-water-609406.
5. Dina Spector, "Here's How Many Days a Person Can Survive Without Water," *Business Insider*, March 8, 2018, https://www.businessinsider.com/how-many-days-can-you-survive-without-water-2014-5.
6. Alina Bradford, "Facts About Tardigrades," LiveScience, July 14, 2017, https://www.livescience.com/57985-tardigrade-facts.html.
7. "Clouds," Weather Wiz Kids, accessed August 7, 2018, http://www.weatherwizkids.com/weather-clouds.htm.

■ Chapter 2
Oil, Water, and Soap

1. "Difference Between Hydrophilic and Hydrophobic," Difference Between, accessed September 6, 2018, http://www.differencebetween.net/science/difference-between-hydrophilic-and-hydrophobic.

Chemistry in Your Everyday Life

2. "Soaps & Detergent: Prehistoric to Middle Ages," American Cleaning Institute, accessed September 1, 2018, https://www.cleaninginstitute.org/clean_living/soaps__detergent_history.aspx.
3. Michael Klopfer, "Frying, Boiling, and the Maillard Reaction," Science Fare, June 1, 2011, https://ediblesciencefaire.wordpress.com/2011/06/01/maillard-reaction.
4. "What Temperature Does the Maillard Reaction Occur?" Seasoned Advice, accessed September 6, 2018, https://cooking.stackexchange.com/questions/29926/what-temperature-does-the-maillard-reaction-occur.
5. "Soaps & Detergents: Chemistry (Surfactants)," American Cleaning Institute, accessed September 3, 2018, https://www.cleaninginstitute.org/clean_living/soaps__detergents_chemistry_2.aspx.
6. "Simple Science: The Difference Between Soap and Detergent," Simple Science by Nyco, accessed September 7, 2018, https://www.nycoproducts.com/news/simple-science-the-difference-between-soap-and-detergent.

■ Chapter 3
Sugars, Sodas, and Diet

1. Julie T. Millard, *Adventures in Chemistry* (Boston, MA: Houghton Mifflin Company, 2008), pp. 232-233.
2. "Simple Sugars: Fructose, Glucose, and Sucrose," Lab Cat, accessed September 22, 2018, https://cdavies.wordpress.com/2009/01/27/simple-sugars-fructose-glucose-and-sucrose.
3. "Starch," BBC Bitesize, accessed November 15, 2018, http://www.bbc.co.uk/bitesize/standard/chemistry/plasticsandothermaterials/carbohydrates/revision/5.
4. "High Fructose Corn Syrup Questions and Answers," U.S. Food & Drug Administration, updated January 4, 2018, https://www.fda.gov/food/ingredientspackaginglabeling/foodadditivesingredients/ucm324856.htm.
5. "Sugar Substitutes and Artificial Sweeteners Chemical Structure," Scientific Psychic, accessed September 16, 2018, https://www.scientificpsychic.com/fitness/artificial-sweeteners.html.
6. "Metabolism," TeensHealth, accessed September 17, 2018, https://kidshealth.org/en/teens/metabolism.html.
7. Bethany Fong, "Do Teens Have Different Nutritional Needs Than Adults?" SFGate, updated July 20, 2017, https://healthyeating.sfgate.com/teens-different-nutritional-needs-adults-2456.html.
8. Thomas R. Rybolt, *Soda Pop Science Projects: Experiments with Carbonated Soft Drinks* (Berkeley Heights, NJ: Enslow Publishers, 2004), pp. 5-6.
9. "My Plate," U.S. Department of Agriculture, accessed September 18, 2018, https://www.choosemyplate.gov.

Chapter Notes

10. Rosane Oliveira, "The Big Picture: Understanding How Nutrients Work Together," UC Davis Integrative Medicine, August 11, 2015, https://ucdintegrativemedicine.com/2015/08/the-big-picture-understanding-how-nutrients-work-together/#gs.gudrZel.
11. "What Are Phytonutrients?" Fruits & Veggies More Matters, accessed September 18, 2018, https://www.fruitsandveggiesmorematters.org/what-are-phytochemicals.

■ Chapter 4
Gases and Our Ocean of Air

1. "Composition of Air," ScienceStruck, accessed August 4, 2018, https://sciencestruck.com/composition-of-air.
2. Paul B. Kelter, James D. Carr, and Andrew Scott, *Chemistry: A World of Choices* (New York, NY: WCB/McGraw-Hill, 1999), pp. 358–359.
3. "How to Achieve the Perfect Bike Tire Pressure," Bicycling Bikes & Gear Training News, accessed August 7, 2018, https://www.bicycling.com/repair/a20004232/how-to-achieve-the-perfect-bike-tire-pressure.
4. "What Is Photosynthesis?" Smithsonian Science Education Center, accessed August 7, 2018, https://ssec.si.edu/stemvisions-blog/what-photosynthesis.
5. "Antoine-Laurent Lavoisier Biography," ThoughtCo., accessed August 7, 2018, https://www.thoughtco.com/antoine-laurent-lavoisier-biography-606881.
6. "Antoine-Laurent Lavoisier," Science History Institute, accessed November 15, 2018, https://wwwsciencehistory.org/historical-profile/antoine-laurent-lavoisier.
7. "Why Do Apple Slices Turn Brown After Being Cut?" *Scientific American*, accessed August 7, 2018, https://www.scientificamerican.com/article/experts-why-cut-apples-turn-brown.
8. Anne Marie Helmenstine, PhD, "How Rust and Corrosion Work," ThoughtCo., updated June 16, 2018, https://www.thoughtco.com/how-rust-works-608461.
9. Robert C. Mebane and Thomas R. Rybolt, *Air and Other Gases* (New York, NY: Twenty-First Century Books, 1995), pp. 12–15.

■ Chapter 5
Metals

1. Chris Woodford, "Mirrors–the Science of Reflection," Explain That Stuff, accessed September 20, 2018, https://www.explainthatstuff.com/howmirrorswork.html.

Chemistry in Your Everyday Life

2. Michael L. Free, "Why Doesn't Stainless Steel Rust?" *Scientific American*, accessed November 15, 2018, https://www.scientificamerican.com/article/why-doesnt-stainless-stee.
3. Sam Kean, "The Sort of Sad Death of the Mercury Thermometer," March 1, 2011, Blogging the Periodic Table, Slate, accessed September 20, 2018, http://www.slate.com/articles/health_and_science/elements/features/2010/blogging_the_periodic_table/the_sort_of_sad_death_of_the_mercury_thermometer.html.
4. "Conductor," WhatIs.com, accessed September 20, 2018, https://whatis.techtarget.com/definition/conductor.
5. "Conductors and Insulators," HyperPhysics Georgia State University, accessed September 20, 2018, http://hyperphysics.phy-astr.gsu.edu/hbase/electric/conins.html.
6. "What Is Heat Conduction?" Phys.org, accessed Sept 20, 2018, https://phys.org/news/2014-12-what-is-heat-conduction.html.
7. "Insulation," Science Learning Hub, Curious Minds, accessed Sept 20, 2018, https://www.sciencelearn.org.nz/resources/1006-insulation.

■ Chapter 6
Polymers, Plastics, and Fabrics

1. "The Basics: Polymer Definition and Properties," American Chemistry Council, accessed November 16, 2018, https://plastics.americanchemistry.com/plastics/The-Basics.
2. "Leo Hendrick Baekeland and the Invention of Bakelite," American Chemical Society, updated October 24, 2013, https://www.acs.org/content/acs/en/education/whatischemistry/landmarks/bakelite.html.
3. "Polymers Up Close and Personal," Polymer Learning Center, Macrogalleria, accessed October 4, 2018, https://pslc.ws/macrog/floor2.htm.
4. "Lifecycle of a Plastic Product," American Chemistry Council, accessed November 16, 2018, https://plastics.americanchemistry.com/Lifecycle-of-a-Plastic-Product.
5. Thomas R. Rybolt and Robert C. Mebane, *Environmental Experiments About Land* (Hillside, NJ: Enslow Publishers, 1993), pp. 62–66.
6. "Thermosets vs. Thermoplastics," Modor Plastics, accessed October 4, 2018, https://www.modorplastics.com/plastics-learning-center/thermoset-vs-thermoplastics.
7. Ann Marie Somma, "Charles Goodyear and the Vulcanization of Rubber," Connecticut History, accessed October 4, 2018, https://connecticuthistory.org/charles-goodyear-and-the-vulcanization-of-rubber.
8. "Man-Made Synthetic Fibers," O Ecotextiles, accessed October 4, 2018, https://oecotextileswordpress.com/2010/07/07/man-made-synthetic-fibers.

Chapter Notes

9. Dominique Mosbergen, "The Oceans Are Drowning in Plastic—and No One's Paying Attention," May 12, 2017, HuffPost, https://www.huffingtonpost.com/entry/plastic-waste-oceans_us_58fed37be4b0c46f0781d426.
10. M. Dochia, "Cotton Fibers" Science Direct, accessed October 4, 2018, https://www.sciencedirect.com/topics/materials-science/cotton-fibers.
11. "Polyester Properties, Production, Price, Market and Uses," Plastics Insight, accessed October 4, 2018, https://www.plasticsinsight.com/resin-intelligence/resin-prices/polyester.

■ Chapter 7
Energy, Carbon Dioxide, and Global Warming

1. "Combustion Reactions in Chemistry," ThoughtCo., accessed September 20, 2018, https://www.thoughtco.com/combustion-reactions-604030.
2. "How Fire Works," How Stuff Works, accessed September 15, 2018, https://science.howstuffworks.com/environmental/earth/geophysics/fire1.htm.
3. "What Are Fossil Fuels?" Belco, accessed November 16, 2018, https://belco.bm/index.php/education-86/what-are-fossil-fuels.
4. "The Ocean and the Carbon Cycle," Science Learning Hub, accessed September 24, 2018, https://www.sciencelearn.org.nz/resources/689the-ocean-and-the-carbon-cycle.
5. "Ocean Acidification," National Oceanic and Atmospheric Administration, accessed September 24, 2018, https://www.noaa.gov/resource-collections/ocean-acidification.
6. "What Is the Greenhouse Effect?" NASA Climate Kids, accessed September 24, 2018, https://climatekids.nasa.gov/greenhouse-effect.
7. "CO_2 on Path to Cross 400 ppm Threshold for a Month," Climate Central, accessed August 4, 2018, http://www.climatecentral.org/news/co2-on-path-to-cross-400-ppm-threshold-for-a-month-17189.
8. Thomas R. Rybolt and Robert C. Mebane, *Environmental Science Fair Projects* (Berkeley Heights, NJ: Enslow Publishers, 2010), pp. 52–55.

atom A building block particle from which everything around us is made.

cation A positively charged atom or molecule.

electron A type of relatively light, negative particle that surrounds the center, or nucleus, and gives an atom its size.

greenhouse effect The trapping of heat due to the blocking of heat energy that would otherwise be radiated or go out into space.

hydrogen bonding A special type of attraction between a somewhat positive hydrogen atom on one molecule to a somewhat negative nitrogen, oxygen, or fluorine atom on a different molecule.

hydrophilic Describes molecules that are attracted to water molecules and mix well with water. Hydrophilic means "water-loving."

hydrophobic Describes molecules that are not attracted to water and do not mix with water. Hydrophobic means "water-fearing."

ion An atom or molecule that has either a positive or negative charge.

macronutrients Foods such as proteins, carbohydrates, and fats required in large amounts in people's diets.

micronutrients Foods such as minerals (metals), vitamins, and plant compounds called phytonutrients that are only required in small amounts in people's diets.

Glossary

molecule A tightly bound collection of atoms that have unique properties and behaviors based on the three-dimensional arrangement of these atoms.

neutron A type of neutral particle found in the nucleus of an atom.

nonpolar Describes molecules that are not polar and so do not have a more positive side and a more negative side.

nucleus The center of an atom.

polar Describes molecules having a more positive side and a more negative side.

polymer A large molecule made of many repeated small molecules (monomers) that are linked together.

proton A type of positive particle found in the nucleus of an atom.

surfactant A molecule with a hydrophilic part (often with a positive or negative charge) and a longer hydrophobic part. Soaps and detergents are types of surfactants.

thermoplastic A plastic that can be heated to soften and then reshape into new objects.

thermoset plastic A plastic that undergoes a chemical reaction when first formed and can't be heated to soften and reshape.

Books

Callery, Sean, and Miranda Smith. *The Periodic Table*. New York, NY: Scholastic Nonfiction, 2017.

Connolly, Sean. *The Book of Ingeniously Daring Chemistry: 24 Experiments for Young Scientists*. New York, NY: Workman Publishing, 2018.

Gardner, Robert, and Joshua Conklin. *Experiments for Future Chemists*. New York, NY: Enslow Publishing, 2016.

Hirschmann, Kris. *The Sticky, Stinky Science Book*. Lake Forest, CA: QEB Publishing, 2018.

Parker, Bertha Morris. *Matter, Molecules, and Atoms*. Ithaca, NY: Yesterday's Classics, 2018.

Websites

American Chemical Society: Adventures in Chemistry
www.acs.org/content/acs/en/education/whatischemistry/adventures-in-chemistry.html

Conduct experiments, play games, and learn more about the chemistry of everyday stuff.

Khan Academy: Chemistry
www.khanacademy.org/science/chemistry

Dive deeper into atoms, elements, chemical reactions, and other chemistry topics.

ThoughtCo.: What Is a Molecule?
www.thoughtco.com/what-is-a-molecule-definition-examples-608506

Read more about molecules and find links to other chemistry topics and activities.

Index

A
acesulfame potassium, 23
aluminum (Al), 35
amino acid, 18
argon (Ar), 28
artificial sweeteners, 23
atmosphere, 28, 48-50
atoms, 4-7

B
Bakelite, 41

C
calcium carbonate, 48
calories, 23
carbon, 6, 8
carbon dioxide, 9, 25, 27-29, 48-51
carbon steel, 35
carbohydrates, 25
carbonated drinks, 25, 27
cations, 36
caustic soda, 19
cellulose, 43-44, 48
chemical bond, 8-9
chemical reactions, 4, 7, 29, 31
chloride, 6
chromium, 35

Coca-Cola (coke), 25
combustion, 48
complex carbohydrates, 21
conductor, 36-37
copper (Cu), 35
cotton, 43-47

D
density, 15
dinitrogen oxide, 28

E
electron, 5-7
energy, 23-25

F
fuel, 48

G
global warming, 48-51
glucose, 22, 29-30
gold (Au), 35
Goodyear, Charles, 43
greenhouse effect, 49-54

H
hemoglobin, 32
humidity, 28-29
hydrogen, 6, 8, 10, 14, 19, 48

Chemistry in Your Everyday Life

hydrogen bonding, 10
hydrophillic, 15
hydrophobic, 15

I

ions, 4, 6
iron (Fe), 31-32, 35
iron oxide (rust), 31-32

L

Lavoisier, Antoine, 31
Lavoisier, Mary Anne, 31
Lead (Pb), 35
lithium (Li), 5, 35

M

Maillard reaction, 17
metal alloys, 35
metals, 35-40
methane (CH4), 28
mercury, 36
micronutrients, 26
molecules, 4, 7-8
monomers, 41

N

nucleus, 5
neutron, 5-6
nitrogen, 6, 28

O

oxygen (O2), 6, 8, 14, 28, 48
ozone (O3), 28

P

periodic table, 6
photosynthesis, 29-30, 48-49
phytonutrients, 26
plastics, 40-43
polyamides (nylons), 42
polycarbonate (Lexan), 41-42
polyester, 43-47
polymers, 38, 41-44
polymerization, 41
polypropylene, 42
polyvinyl chloride (PVC), 42
Priestley, Joseph, 31
proton, 5-7

R

rubber, 43

S

silver (Ag), 35
soap, 16-20
sodium hydroxide, 19
stainless steel, 35
sucrose (sugar), 8, 20-21
sulfur dioxide, 9-10,
sufractants, 16-17
synthetic polymer, 41

T

tardigrades (water bears), 11
thermoplastics, 43

V

vulcanization, 42

64